George Edmund] Otis

Thurid, and other poems

George Edmund] Otis

Thurid, and other poems

ISBN/EAN: 9783743335257

Manufactured in Europe, USA, Canada, Australia, Japa

Cover: Foto ©ninafisch / pixelio.de

Manufactured and distributed by brebook publishing software (www.brebook.com)

George Edmund] Otis

Thurid, and other poems

THURID.

PART FIRST.

From Hoffdabrekka's crags, the gray mists drifted
  Before the breath of new awakening day;
From shore and sea, the night cloud slowly lifted,
  And early sunlight rippled on the bay.

'Neath yon bold cliff, rests Headbrink's fruitful valley,
  Its verdant meadows bordered by the strand;
A lovely spot, where south-winds love to dally
  With yielding flowers that bloom on every hand.

Beside the shore, in sunshine basks the village,
    A home for those who plough the northern seas,
A resting place, where, tired of gale and pillage,
    The storm-tossed Viking courts unwonted ease.

With merry shout and song the echoes waking,
    From far and near, beclad in garments gay,
Both old and young their way are hither taking,
    To join in honoring Headbrink's gala day.

The sports begin and all is noise and motion,
    The glad sun smiles upon the jocund scene,
And seems to pause, ere gilding wide the ocean,
    To cheer the dancers on the village green.

With games of strength and skill, the day advances,
    Here wander lovers silent on the strand;
Some, songs intone filled with weird northern fancies,
    Or tell strange stories of some distant land.

Never I ween did joyous crowd assemble
  Such wealth of fresh and merry fair faced
    girls,
Who view delighted the rough sports, nor
    tremble
  At rude encounters of contending churls.

The fairest far among these fairest faces,
  A heavenly face, embodied from a dream,
Her form divine, enshrined in woman's graces,
  Meet subject for the proudest minstrel's
    theme,

Resting apart, within a coppice shady,
  Reclines young Thurid, loveliest of the
    throng,
Joy of her lord, good Thorodd's winsome
    lady,
  Bleak Froda's pride, the queen of many a
    song! —

With weary, absent air, sits Thurid dreaming,
  Her fair hair, loosened, waving in the wind,
And careless gazes at the sports, as seeming
  No pleasure in the noisy mirth to find.

Within her heart, lurks deep some secret sorrow,
  Some untold grief, that time can ne'er erase!
She hates to-day, yet longs not for the morrow,
  And helpless sadness shadows o'er her face.

She longs to roam o'er Froda's broad wastes lonely,
  And leave the jarring laughter of the crowd,
To nurse her grief, where moaning wild winds only
  Discourse of woe, in whispers hoarse and loud.

Still grows the mirth, its merry round unbroken,
  The Muse herself seems mistress of the dance;
And tender thoughts in loving eyes are spoken,
  The heart's pent secrets proffered in a glance.

Wrapped in the dance's tangled, circling
    mazes,
  Or drinking wonders from some Scaldic
      song,
None heed th' approach of one, who anxious
    gazes
  On each fair face that meets him in the
      throng.

Haughty his air and confident his bearing,
  His form instinct with strength and manly
    grace,
His gray eyes speak of cool resolve and dar-
    ing;
  Foreign his garb, and sun-browned is his
      face.

Anon, above the din of revel sounding,
  A growing murmur rises from the crowd,
And leaving sports, the throng press on, sur-
    rounding
  The stranger's form, and cheer him long and
      loud.

With gracious mien, receives he each rude
    greeting,

For few such glad and loud acclaim had
    won,
And proudly hears each mouth the shout re-
    peating,
  "Long life to Biörn, Asbrand's gallant
    son!"

And thus afar, in shady copse reclining,
  Doth Thurid, startled, hear the welcoming
    cry,
And shrinks, as if the cruel truth divining;
  And pales and trembles, though she knows
    not why.

With throbbing heart and quickened breath,
    up starting,
  She notes the sound of footsteps drawing
    near,
And hears a voice, a deeper dread imparting,
  A voice that erst came sweetly to her ear.

In vain she strives to lull her heart's wild
    beating,
  To still her anguish with close clenchèd
    palms,

And calmly tries to wait the dreaded meeting;
  Too late! for Biörn clasps her in his arms.

Entranced they stand, their souls with passion
    teeming,
  The heart's deep longing blazoned on each
    face,
From hungry eyes, a mutual love is gleaming,
  And each lives ages in that short embrace.

A moment, and her pride and conscience
    wielded
  Their conquering might, and Thurid feels
    the sway;
Recalls her will, and, blushing to have yielded,
  With stricken heart, from Biörn breaks
    away.

And, then, though every word her heart is
    rending,
  And seems a dagger to her tortured breast,
In tones where love and blank despair are
    blending,
  With downcast eyes, she Biörn thus ad-
    dressed: —

"The hour has come; the hour replete with
    sorrow,
  This luckless hour, foreseen since long ago!
Ah! would that I an icy soul might borrow,
  To tell, impassive, my dull tale of woe!

"My throbbing heart, love's funeral knell is
    tolling,
  Flown from my breast to fair-haired Frey
    above.
Ah! why did life with tasteless joys cajoling,
  Forsake not Thurid, ere she learned to love!

"'Twas Midgard's work, some devil's charm
    was burning,
  When Biörn trusting left my hapless side!
Some cruel god, 'gainst me his wrath was
    turning
  And strangled Truth, to make me Thorodd's
    bride!

"Aye! start not Biörn, every word is wound-
    ing
  The breast of Thurid, deeper than thine own,

Then calm thy soul, and curb thy blood's mad
    bounding !
My hand is his ; my heart is thine alone !

" Slow dragged the hours, when Biörn sadly
    left me,
But gladly dwelt I on his quick return,
When came the words that of all hope bereft
    me,
And bade me then my broken heart inurn.

" They said, 'gainst odds, thou'dst fallen,
    bravely fighting,
And died the foremost in th' unequal fray !
I heard their tale, my very life-blood blighting,
    And called on Death to shroud my willing
    clay.

" But grim-faced Hela, all my prayers un-
    heeding,
No welcome becked me with her icy hand.
My murky star, not e'en that boon conceding,
    Refused me respite in that unknown land.

" Month dragged on month, my broken heart
    benumbing,

And maddened grief to still despair had
    grown.
'Twas then my soul seemed soothed by Tho-
    rodd's coming,
Who silent sat, or spoke of thee alone.

" His time-worn face, th' unwonted color
    mounting,
  He'd speak thy praises, tell of combats
    won;
And long would sit, some gallant deed re-
    counting,
  And mourned thy loss, as though thou wert
    his son.

" A year passed on, and Autumn days were
    waning,
  Bare waved the branches of the tree-tops old,
The clouds hung low; the chill winds moaned
    complaining,
  And dead leaves whispered of the coming
    cold.

" Then Thorodd seated by the warm fire bask-
    ing,

In the bleak twilight asked me for my hand.
'Thy heart is dead,' he said. 'and past the asking,
　Then grant the first, which is at thy command.

"'I ask a boon, all powerless of returning,
　To her who hears me, aught save age and pain,
A hearth whereon no cheerful fire is burning,
　And barren halls where joy can ne'er remain.

"'Of my own heart, I speak not in my pleading,
　'Twere naught to thee, to know it were thine own;
I only say, my life, my soul is needing
　But Thurid's self; I ask for that alone.'

"'Gainst what he begged, my inmost soul contended,
　And vainly sought I anger to essay,
My heavy brain no fair excuse extended,
　And blinded Duty pointed out the way!

" On Thorodd's care and kindness uncom-
plaining,
And love for thee, my grateful thoughts
were bent,
For that alone, a cheerful presence feigning,
With heavy heart, I gave a loth consent.

" 'Twere wanton pain, to rack thy heart in
dwelling
On that cursed time, which made me Thorodd's wife,
My very tongue shrinks palsied from the tell-
ing!
Oh! darkest day in Thurid's darksome life!

" One boisterous night, when winds blew shrill
and dreary,
And owls, storm-blinded, hooted from the
walls,
Two strangers came, all travel-stained and
weary,
To ask for shelter in dark Froda's halls.

" And when about the blazing back-log seated,
They said they came from wave-washed
Jomsburg fair,

Wild stories told, and once thy name re-
    peated,
  And called thee leader of the Vikings there.

"'Then Biörn lives!' I cried, in haste up-
    starting,
  But straightway swooning on the cold floor
    fell,
  Yet faintly heard, while sense was yet depart-
    ing,
  'The Viking Biörn is alive and well.'

"For weeks unconscious, on a sick-bed lying,
  Those dark words tinged each fever painted
    dream,
  How happy to have gained repose in dying,
  And drunk oblivion from Death's sullen
    stream.

"But life's curst fire, within me feebly burn-
    ing,
  Waxed slowly stronger, growing on despair:
  And then the thought of thee, some day re-
    turning,
  Oppressed my soul and left its burden
    there!

"Since then no joy or cheerful thought has
    blended
  With th' unstilled anguish of my aching
      heart,
My task is done; my weary tale is ended,
  And cruel Fate decrees that we must part!"

All dazed at what he hears, is Biörn standing;
  Nor heeds, at once, that Thurid's plaint is
      o'er.
And wonders, when his faltering speech com-
      manding,
  He hears his voice, in tones unheard before!

"Thurid," he said, "thy damnèd tale has
      chilled me;
  Thou'st forced the wonted life blood from
      my heart,
Far kinder had it been, if thou hadst killed
      me,
  Or hidden from me, what thou sayst thou
      art!

"I will not wound thee now with vain re-
      proaches,

A sinewy soul exists not in the past,
But lives on what's to come, and ne'er en-
    croaches
  On Fate's dread game, to mourn the die
    that's cast.

" Not idle tears, but brave, unflinching action,
  Make reparation for an evil done;
Then rouse thyself, and prove thy proud ex-
    traction
  From princely blood, and victory is won.

" When, long ago, my heart and troth were
    deeded
  In prized exchange for word and love of
    thine,
No foolish form or meddling priest was
    needed
  To bind our souls, or make thy being mine!

" Our love itself was warrant for our loving!
  Our first warm kiss was registered above;
For nuptial rite, the smiling gods approving
  Looked from the clouds, and marked the
    seal of love!

2

"Then think thee, Thurid, naught that is can
 sever
 That binding marriage, hallowed in its
 power!
Mine thou art only, now, and e'en forever,
 In th' unknown life, that borders death's
 dark hour!

"Thou lov'st not Thorodd; 'twas but erring
 duty
 That stirred thy pity for that dotard gray.
He needs it not! — Then blight not love and
 beauty
 With drivelling cares, nor waste youth's
 fleeting day.

"But o'er the seas, where other stars are shin-
 ing
 O'er other lands, than this by far more fair,
We'll sink the past, and leave all vain repin-
 ing,
 And wealth of love shall be our only care!

"Then fly with me, to where my bark is riding

Off green Raunhaven's stormless rock-bound
    bay,
And once embarked, to favoring winds confid-
    ing,
Another sun will find us far away!"

" Ask me not, Biörn! Here in tears entreat-
    ing,
Hear me conjure thee : leave me here alone!
For only thee, my tired heart is beating,
To Thorodd wed, my love is all thine own.

" Yet whispering conscience speaks its ready
    warning,
And sadly says, our lives must lie apart, —
And bids me wait, through weary days of
    mourning,
Till welcome death unites us, heart to
    heart!"

O'er Biörn's brow the angry blood is rushing,
As Thurid speaks; yet silently he stands,

While every word each lingering hope is
    crushing,
  And thwarted passion all his soul com-
    mands.

" A love that falters in its goal's attaining,
  Or hesitates when coward conscience calls,
Is basely weak, and matters not the gaining !
  A bloodless love, that e'en its goal appalls !

" Thou know'st thy heart, and doubtless thou
    hast taken
  The course thy cautious reason deems most
    fair, —
I laud thy sense of duty all unshaken,
  And leave thee, false one, to thy Thorodd's
    care."

And e'en ere Thurid calms her heart's mad
    beating,
  Or ere her voice one answering word has
    found,
She hears his foot-fall die away, retreating,
  And moaning low, falls swooning to the
    ground !

Back draws the crowd, as Biörn onward pressing,
  With hurrying step, and dark, forbidding mien,
To those around, no farewell word addressing,
  Heeds not the throng, and hastens from the scene!

A misty line, Raunhaven's shore is sinking,
  The bark breasts onward with the urging blast,
She swiftly flies, and league to league is linking,
  Till e'en the headlands drop from sight at last.

In Froda's halls a moaning woman wanders
  The whole night long, nor seems to think of rest,
But tearless walks, with vacant air, and ponders
  On some dull grief that racks her aching breast.

PART SECOND.

The firelight, bright and ruddy, fell
   On oaken beam and blackened wall,
And wavering, faint, anon would swell
   In radiant glow throughout the hall,
With color warm, that came and went,
A phantom blush o'er darkness sent!

Through scarce closed shutters found its way
   A pale moon-beam of frozen light;
All pure and motionless it lay,
   A soul it seemed from the outer night,
Far wandering on some mission blest,
Here resting as the fire-light's guest.

Refined and calm, though from the same
   Wild fiery cause, serene it lay,
And coldly watched the baser flame
   At savage sport on the hearth-stone gray,
And gave fresh tone to the silvered hair
Of the sad-faced woman crouching there.

Alone she sat, with absent eyes
   Fixed on the glowing coals intent,

And watched the red flames fall and rise,
   'Mid mounting sparks that came and went,
With bended brow and drooping head,
Tracing the past in th' embers red.

Dreamy summers in green array,
   Dreary winters with biting cold,
Slowly, sadly, had passed away,
   Leaving her loveless, hopeless, and old,
Longing for death as the only goal
Of rest and sleep for her weary soul.

Looking back through the mist of years,
   Gloomy vista of pain and care,
Sees she her young heart drowned in tears,
   Pining for bliss that she may not share,
Forbidden to love where she loves alone,
Filled with a passion she dare not own.

Sees she herself, enchained for life,
   Hampered in bonds by duty sealed,
Widowed her heart, while yet a wife,
   Feigning a love which she cannot yield ;
And sees the lover she thought had died,
Returning at last to claim his bride !

Coming, to find her newly wed,
  Entrapped, betrayed, by false report;
Cruel the parting words he said,
  And angered, left her with anguish fraught,
To wail her fate, and to curse the power
That ruled the chance of her natal hour!

He left her thus, and not one word,
  Or hopeful sign, or token fair,
Had e'er been sent by him, or heard,
  To tell her e'en he lived and where.
She only knew, in by-gone years
He left her there, alone, in tears!

She saw the ashes spread below
  The hissing logs from whence they came,
As pure and white as virgin snow,
  Yet tinged with red by the flick'ring flame;
Beheld a husband, fond though stern,
A slighted love, a funeral urn.

With widowed heart and widowed hand,
  In lonely state at Froda's hall,
She weary notes the waning sand
  From out her glass engulfèd fall,

And sees unmoved, that day by day,
Her faint strength sinks in slow decay.

While lost in reveries sad like these,
    Unnoticed comes the noise without
Of bolts withdrawn and rattling keys,
    And stranger's voice in answering shout,
And heavy footsteps drawing near, —
Yet naught awakes her sleeping ear.

And not till foot-falls struck the floor,
    And strangers stood within the room,
Did Thurid gain herself once more
    And peering toward the dusky gloom
That shades the doorway, strives to rise,
And asks their aim with anxious eyes.

Rough men they were, but with an air
    That marked their hearts of gentler mould ;
A front that bade the foe beware !
    An open mien that plainly told
Of soul unstained and guileless mind,
Revengeful foes, yet friends o'er kind !

In seamen's garb they both were clad,
    On faces brown they bore the trace

Of wind and sun, and each one had
    A bearing proud, and easy grace,
That spoke the habit of command,
And marked the chief on sea or land.

"My brother and myself are here," —
    Thus spoke the foremost of the pair,
Who seemed the elder, drawing near, —
    "To doff the load that now we bear
Of duty to a distant friend.
This brings us hither, this our end.

"Our story strange is shortly told:
    Some two years since, by adverse gales,
We lost the course we sought to hold,
    The savage North-wind caught our sails,
And tore them on the bending mast,
And bore us powerless on the blast.

"O'er countless leagues of angry sea,
    We bore to southward, and for days
The murky heavens lent no key
    Of guiding stars or slanting rays
Of fiery sun, to show us where
Upon the trackless waste we were.

" We drifted onward, ever on;
   And when at last we hoped no more,
And in despair sat tired and wan,
   We dimly traced a line of shore,
One moment hid by mist and rain,
Then faintly peering out again.

" And now when every heart was cheered,
   The gale grew faint with wasted strength,
The warming sun at last appeared,
   And showed the coast-line stretch its length
In rocky headlands, bluff and high,
Till distance screened them from the eye.

" We looked upon a shore unknown,
   And gazed entrancèd at the line
Of verdant hills with trees o'ergrown,
   And rocky ledges fringed with pine;
Each moment some green wonder drew
Our eager eyes, and cheered our view.

" We found a haven smooth and fair;
   But scarce had reached the welcome strand,
Ere crowding on, with flowing hair
   And brazen skins, a savage band

Of shouting men, with hostile mien,
Sprang on us from each covert green!

" O'erborne by numbers, we were bound
    With leathern cords, and made to wait,
Close tied and cramped upon the ground,
    Until the chief decreed our fate;
And bade us either live as slaves,
Or tortured sink to welcome graves!

" Ere long an aged man drew nigh;
    Of paler hue, unlike the rest,
With eyes deep set and forehead high,
    And snowy beard upon his breast;
A mien majestic, carriage free, —
He seemed a man of high degree.

" He scanned us o'er with kindly eyes,
    And spoke to us in barb'rous tongue;
And answering not, to our surprise,
    He asked what strange mischance had flung
Our bark on this remotest strand,
In th' accents of our native land!

" And when our wondrous tale was told,
    And who we were, and whence we came,

Adown his cheek the tear-drop rolled,
　And pity shook his aged frame;
And turning to the savage horde,
He bade them cut each binding cord.

" Long weeks we tarried with our friend,
　Who asked us o'er and o'er again
About ourselves, and e'er would lend
　An anxious ear and eager brain
Whene'er we spoke of Iceland's shore,
And homes we thought to see no more!

" We vainly asked him in our turn,
　About himself, and whence he came,
His early life; but ne'er could learn;
　His answer always came the same:
' Seek not to rouse the buried years,
Let memory rest and dry her tears!'

" Meantime we strove to fit again
　Our bark to breast the angry wave,
And bear us homeward o'er the main,
　Or else to grant one common grave,
So that together we might die!
Together join the gods on high!

"While thus we toiled, a fever dire
   Brought low the life-blood of our friend;
With troubled brain, and veins on fire,
   He felt approach the clouded end
Of life's entanglement of woe
And joys we dream of, never know!

"And when the rank disease had run
   Its burning course, his weary breath
Betokened that his work was done,
   And told him to prepare for death;
And straightway then, ere yet he died,
He bade me hasten to his side: —

"'While yet my laboring breath remains
   To frame my thought,' he faintly said,
'And ere my fading reason wanes,
   And strangers lay me with their dead,
A kindness I would ask of thee,
To bear a token o'er the sea;

"'If faithless Fortune should be kind,
   And guide thee to thy native shore,
I, dying, bid thee strive to find
   A lady fair, who dwelt of yore

At Froda, on the rugged way
That leads to fair Raunhaven's Bay.

" 'Her name is Thurid; if she live,
   I charge thee bear to her this ring,
And with it but this message give, —
   " To Thurid would this bauble bring
Remembrance of her plighted word, —
To wed the one her heart preferred."

" 'Or, if beneath the heather fair
   You find she rests, search out the place
Wherein she lies, and set it there
   Amid the flowers that chance to grace
That holy spot, wherein doth rest
That loving heart, that guileless breast!'

" And as he spoke, he feebly took
   From off his hand a ring of gold,
And gave it to me with a look
   Of glad relief, that sadly told
He feared not now th' approach of death,
Nor wished to stay his fainting breath!

" I never heard him speak again;
   For now, at last, the favoring breeze,

We long had waited for in vain,
   Arose to urge us o'er the seas;
And bearing eastward from the shore,
We sought our distant land once more.

" 'Twere needless to recount the toil
   And dangers dire through which we passed,
Ere once again our native soil
   We touched, and reached our homes at last;
And nought remains for us to do,
But proffer now this ring to you."

And moving now to where she stands,
   Transfixed and stunned by what he says,
He lays the jewel in her hands;
   She speaks not, but her face betrays,
Though vainly she essays control,
The turmoil of her startled soul;

She silent stands, yet, tearless, tries,
   With lips unanswering, — all in vain, —
To frame the whirling thoughts that rise
   Within her hot and fevered brain.
A chilling languor round her grows,
And o'er her sense a shadow throws!

One moment thus, and then a light
   Unearthly o'er her eyes has passed;
And, rising to her utmost height,
   With quickened breath she speaks at last,
And, pointing to the vacant chair,
She bids them note the figure there.

" He rises now and becks me on!
   I follow, Biörn; frown not so!
Nor look at me so sad and wan;
   I'll follow wheresoe'er you go!
For welcome death comes on apace;
The grave must be our trysting-place!

A rigid fixedness, the sign
   Her spirit struggles to be gone,
Constrains each lineament, and line
   Upon her face; — the deathly dawn,
That guides her to a fairer sphere,
Breaks on her vision, pure and clear!

The fire-light waned and faintly fell
   On oaken beam and blackened wall;

No longer does the mistress dwell
　In Froda's bare and dreary hall.
The frozen moonbeam sinks to rest
On Thurid's now o'er quiet breast.

CHARITY.

CHARITY.

PART FIRST.

The hot midsummer sun, that, through the day
Of ardent toil, had slaked his burning thirst
From each cool stream that in his pathway lay,
And drained its current low, now sank immersed
In cool, refreshing clouds, that proudly nursed
The bright remembrance of his kissed good-night,
In flaming glory, various hued, that burst
Upon the eye enraptured at the sight,
And decked the distant hills in mystic radiance bright!

Upon the greensward, sloping to the road,
From where a modest, rude-built cottage stood,
Half hid in flowering vines, a fair abode,
Sits Charity alone, in thoughtful mood,
With absent eyes fixed on the purple hood
Of sunset clouds, which tops the distant
    hills.
The evening song of birds from out the wood
Hard by, a maze of pretty chirps and trills,
With thoughts of wakening love her dream-
    ing spirit fills:

Untouched, beside her, stands the idle wheel;
With face upturned and resting on her hand,
Her eyes, unwavering, hazel depths reveal,
That speak of courage and the soul's com-
    mand.
Her rich, brown hair, by twilight breezes
    fanned,
A matchless framing makes for that fair face,
Whereon the rosy hue of health doth stand;
While every line and feature bears the trace
Of inborn gentleness and untaught modest
    grace.

Her simple gown of finest homespun made,
Betrays the contour of a figure rare ;
The silken 'kerchief, o'er her shoulders laid,
A pleasing charm and stolen grace doth wear.
From happy contact with a form so fair !
And, as she sits thus, often doth a sigh
Escape her breast, a sigh not born of care,
An echo merely, which doth soft reply
To longings whispered by a heart where love
    doth lie !

Save nature's harmony, the myriad tones
Of insect wings, and birds, and whisp'ring
    leaves,
And brooklet rippling over moss-grown stones,
No other sound the soothèd ear receives ;
The hour it is, when fancy deftly weaves
Her web impalpable ; with care oppressed,
The weary soul its trammeled life relieves,
Awakes new sense within the burdened breast,
Communes with nature's self, and solace finds
    and rest.

And thus to-night doth Charity confide
Her secret life unto the listening wind

And sun-tinged clouds, nor e'en would seek to hide
Her inmost soul, to new-born love inclined;
But proffers all, nor leaves one thought behind.
Her dreamy fancy leads her, unrestrained,
And paints bright pictures, vague and undefined,
Yet all with glowing colors bright ingrained,
Where only trusting love and gladness are contained.

While thus intent on meditations sweet
And deep, her soul in blissful thought lies drowned,
She does not heed the sound of horse's feet,
That, faintly heard at first, now nearer sound,
And wake the sleeping echoes all around.
But when, at last, she notes the thudding tread
Of hoofs, now close, upon the dusty ground,
She strives to rise, and, startled, turns her head,
While, coursing o'er her cheeks, the rosy blushes spread.

And, drawing near, the horseman checks his
　　pace,
And brings his steed upon the roadside green,
And guides him, all impatient, toward the
　　place
Where Charity doth sit; and then with mien
Wherein far more than bare regard is seen,
He gayly greets her, and she doth return
His salutation with a smile serene,
Yet blushes deeper, lest he should discern
Her crimsoned cheeks, which now with height-
　　ened color burn.

The rider, Wilmot Lee, upon his brow
Bears stamped the token, clear and well-de-
　　fined,
That marks the one whom nature doth endow
With kindly heart and unsuspecting mind; —
A man whose every instinct is refined, —
By fortune favored, from his birth, with place
And health and wealth and all that is inclined
To dull the soul, and sympathy efface,
He, modest, wears them all with decency and
　　grace.

That something indefinable in line
Of feature and of form, — that nameless air
Which speaks the gentleman inborn, the sign
Of race, and breeding high, and culture rare,
His presence all unconsciously doth wear.
His riding-coat, close fitting, doth betray
A large, yet well-knit frame; his shoulders square,
And broad, deep chest, a latent strength display,
A figure nobly built and formed of noble clay!

So closely every movement of his steed
He lightly follows, that it seems his own.
The horse, with full, wide breast, and limbs for speed
Well made, and wiry neck, well upward thrown,
And chestnut-coat, that sleek and lustrous shone,
Seemed worthy of the load he lightly bore.
He needed but the rider's voice alone
To speed him on, or check; to him 'twas law,
And stinging spurs or lash could urge him on no more.

The rider's eyes and Charity's express,
In one short, earnest, heart-disclosing glance,
A shrinking love that neither dares confess;
And then, in tones whose softness doth enhance
The import of the idle words which chance
And random thought suggest, with stifled sighs,
They talk of trifles! In a happy trance
Of love-lit thought, with tender, downcast
    eyes,
She sits. All earth seems fair, and cloudless
    seem the skies!

How slight a substance hath the fairest joy,
When, with the breath that frames some triv-
    ial word,
Is blasted all the scanty, thin alloy
Of happiness, we idly dreamed secured,
And nought remains but worthless dross!
    Deep stirred,
With sudden grief the stricken soul is rife,
At some light, careless speech; and sees de-
    ferred
The hope of freedom from its wonted strife!
For thus do trifles touch our hidden, inmost
    life!

And so, when Wilmot said he must be gone,
As, ere he slept that night, before him lay,
O'er rough and lonely roads, but little worn,
A ride to Boston, many miles away;
And answering Charity, whose eyes convey
A look of curiosity; "I go,"
He said, "to seek a ship within the bay,
That sails for England!" All the joyous glow
Forsook her heart, and checked her pulse's
    happy flow!

"The urgent voice of friends from o'er the sea,
And cares forgot amid these pleasant scenes,
And hard, exacting duty, all decree
That I should homeward turn. My feeling
    leans
Towards further sojourn mid these leafy screens
Of forest broad and deep, where life is true
And natural; where every kind act means
Regard, and has no further end in view;
But judgment bids me haste to say to all,
    adieu!"

As 'neath the tranquil bosom of the deep,
Wild, boist'rous currents flow, concealed, un-
    known,

Nor wake the surface from its glassy sleep;
So Charity, whose love had, startled, flown,
All trembling, from her eyes, where first it
    shone,
And, wounded, sought its refuge in her heart,
With strange, untaught control, and pride
    alone
In woman found inborn, and native art,
Betrays no token of the pain his words impart!

Nor says she aught at first; and by no sign
That speaks surprise, or troubled look, is
    shown
The sudden turmoil of the thoughts that line
Her fevered heart; but, finally, in tone
As unconcerned and easy as his own,
She tells him that his many friends will mourn
The absence of a face so newly grown
Familiar; and, to distant shores though gone,
Kind memories of his name will still be freshly
    worn!

On Wilmot's ear, the tenor of her speech
Conventional, falls coldly; and the heart
That he had sought, though all in vain, to
    teach

The lesson stern of duty, all its part
Of forced control forgets, and newly start
The pent-up fires of love within his breast!
The very tones, which, by her ready art
Of self-command, had chilled his ear, impressed,
Perversely, all his heart with added warmth
    and zest!

And lest his love, new lighted, should enforce
Its fair avowal, and his purpose stay,
He hastens to be gone, his sole resource,
And, as he lifts his rein and rides away, —
" 'Twere little need to bid farewell to-day,"
He says, " To-morrow evening, once again,
I shall return, to spend the prized delay
Among these well-loved friends, ere o'er the
    main
My good ship sails, and shores of fair New
    England wane!"

A moment more, and he is lost to sight,
Amid the deepening shades, and but the beat
Of hoofs breaks on the stillness of the night,
And fainter, further grows! The sounds repeat,

In dying cadence, to her soul replete
With woe, each word her ear but now received.
" And thus doth end the foolish, fond conceit,
The idle dream of love my fancy weaved!
Thy course is run, poor heart, thy sorry goal
    achieved!"

And thus communing with herself, distraught
And sick at heart, sits Charity; the rein
With which her maiden pride so long had
    sought
To check all outward token of the pain
Within her breast, no longer doth restrain
Its charge; and silent start her heart-wrung
    tears.
The last, soft tints of mellow sun-glow wane;
Each golden trace of daylight disappears,
While grief, around her heart, its darksome
    barrier rears.

Meanwhile, as through the darkness Wilmot
    speeds,
The thought of Charity, her modest air
And gentle voice, address his heart, which
    pleads

For a return to her he loves, to bear
Assurance of that love.   He does not dare
To listen to its tempting tones, or pause,
Lest he should yield, and even now forswear
His wav'ring purpose, and forget its cause ;
But urges on his steed ; his rein more tightly
  draws !

When sense of duty strong doth prop the will,
The path we follow, e'en though hard and
  rude,
And narrow though its bounds, is lighted still
With sweet approval from the soul ; and,
  viewed
Afar, we see our goal.   No fears intrude
Upon the mind to check our plodding feet !
But let a doubt assail us, then are strewed
Along our way perplexities which cheat
Our sense !   Dark grows the road, and warns
  us to retreat !

Thus far sustained in what he deemed was due
To prejudice of friends, and to the sphere
In which he moved, made of the chosen few
That formed his world, one way alone seemed
  clear.

CHARITY. 49

From early childhood, he was wont to hear
That never love 'twixt high and low degree
Could hope to prosper; and his customed ear
Had early grown, while yet his heart was free,
To hear, unquestioning, society's decree.

No vague suspicion, even that his heart,
For her, could aught save bare regard contain,
Or but a fondest friendship, where no part
Of his soul's deeper warmth should entrance
    gain,
And turn his thoughts to love, had crossed his
    brain.
But when, at length, his hiding heart con-
    fessed
The secret truth, one only course seemed plain,
And straightway he had steeled his troubled
    breast,
From her he vainly loved, to part, with soul
    oppressed.

And not till now, when riding through the
    night,
And fresh from converse with his love, alone,
4

With time for thought, do doubts, uneasy, blight
His earnest strength of purpose! Now come blown
Across the mirror of his mind, where shone
His duty's image, questionings and fears,
Until its shining surface is o'ergrown
With gathering mist, and, clouded, naught appears
Save the faint picture of his wounded love in tears!

He harder rides, and vainly, would escape
The dark suspicion that his judgment erred
In urging him to fly, and tries to shape
And prop once more his shaken purpose, blurred
And weakened by the flitting doubts that stirred
Within his troubled brain. A settled frown
Is on his brow, and whispers faintly heard
That 'scape his heart, and say, Return, weigh down
His soul. And thus oppressed he nears the lighted town!

PART SECOND.

The sweet-breathed dawn, that comes with
    rustling feet
To guide the new-born day, in whispers low
Bids sleeping Charity arise and greet
The early sun! No token doth she show
Of the salt, burning tears, which needs must
    flow
Ere she could sink to rest, but with a mind
Made up to bear with cheerfulness the blow
Her heart had suffered, she doth rise, inclined
To bravely meet whate'er may be her fate,
    resigned!

With even brow and ever cheerful mien,
She minds her simple round of household cares,
And sings, while at her task; then, on the
    green
Before the door, when all is done, she bears
Once more her spinning gear, and, heedful,
    spares
No idle moment, ere she deftly plies
The droning wheel. And thus, the long day
    wears

Itself away. Her heart and courage rise
And gain new strength, as each full, busy moment flies.

It is not that all pain has left her breast, —
A sorrow doth not fade so soon and die, —
It still lies rooted there; yet though op-
 pressed
And sad her soul, with resolution high
She stills her grief, and stifles every sigh,
And, uncomplaining, strives her part to bear;
And, though one dearest source of joy is dry,
She earnest seeks to find all else more fair
Than e'er before, and full of beauties new and
 rare!

The brightest time, by far, in all the day,
For Charity, was when, his labor through,
Her father, in the afternoon, his way
Towards home would weary wend. She ever
 grew
Impatient, as the hour approached, and knew
The very moment, from long habitude,
At which, unerringly, he homeward drew;
The hill top, o'er which crept the road, she
 viewed

With watchful eyes, her heart with fondest
    love imbued.

And when, at last, she saw him mount the
    hill,
She hastened on to greet him, and returned,
Her hand in his, as she had done when still
A child; and when her instinct quick dis-
    cerned
He seemed well pleased with what the day had
    turned
To his account, and that his brow was clear,
She asked him of the farm, and grew con-
    cerned
In mention of the work, and then would hear
Him talk of fruitful fields, and crops, with
    eager ear.

But when he met her with a smile that shone
But on his lips, and came not from his heart,
She spoke not of the fields, and sought alone
To soothe and cheer him, and would strive to
    start
His mind toward fairer thoughts, and far
    apart

From rustic cares. And when their homely
 meal
Is o'er, beside him sits, and tasks each art
To please ; and reads the Golden Book to heal
His troubled soul, till shades of twilight round
 them steal.

And so to-night she waits for him. — The hour
Has overrun, and just within the door
She waiting stands, and anxious doth devour,
With straining eyes, the roadway o'er and
 o'er ;
Yet still he comes not. — Never yet before,
Had she, thus all impatient, watched in vain
To see him top the hill, and ever more
She fears and wonders what strange tangled
 train
Of hind'ring circumstance, his steps can thus
 detain.

Yet now a sound of hoofs and jangling chains
Is faintly heard, and from a dusty cloud
That, like a beacon's warning smoke, slow
 trains
Behind him, speeding with his body bowed

To meet the wind, a rider comes. Dark
        browed,
He presses wildly on, with anxious face;
The road-stained horse, with trace-chains
        clanking loud,
And rude farm harness swinging, shows the
        trace
Of sudden summons, from the fields to fly
        apace.

With foam-flecked bridle strained, he hurries
        by,
Unheeding Charity, — and once again
Are faintly heard, and in the distance die,
The sounds of horse's tread and rattling chain;
She knows the horseman for a yeoman plain,
Who tilled outlying lands some miles away.
Unshaped forebodings dread disturb her
        brain.
The rider's haste, her father's strange delay,
Suggest vague, startling fears, her judgment
        cannot stay.

Some trouble seems on foot! Her spirit grows
Impatient, and rebels at this suspense.

Not overlong has she to wait! There shows,
Once more, far up the road, a dust cloud dense,
That greater grows, and ere her o'erstrained
 sense
Has ceased to hear the horseman in retreat,
Her anxious ear receives with dread intense,
The sounds of jolting wheels, and hurried beat
Of hoofs, that nearer draw, and echo doth re-
 peat.

And down the hill, at headlong, plunging
 speed,
There comes a rude farm wagon, roughly
 drawn
By two tired, panting horses. — Some dire
 need
Must urge them on their way. With mien
 forlorn,
A crouching, dust-stained group is swiftly
 borne
Along, while one tall, stalwart figure guides
The pressing steeds, whose face is pale and
 worn.
Some deeply dark anxiety abides
Within his breast; and, on his brow, black
 trouble rides!

At slackened pace they come, and when abreast
The cottage door, draw up. And then straight-
 way
The driver springs upon the green; the rest,
Meantime, converse in whispers low, while
 stray
Their frightened glances o'er the hill-top gray
Behind them! With a sorely troubled brain,
Wherein relief is mingled with dismay,
She sees, perplexed, her father once again
Draw toward her, with a look he strives to
 hide, in vain.

A look wherein she reads of trouble near,
And yet to come! In husky, hurried tone,
He speaks: " Come, Charity, the way is clear
For us to fly! The road behind is strewn
With dangers dire! All hope of rest is flown
From this dear home. For look towards the
 farm,
Where even now the crackling flames are
 thrown
High heavenward! The long delayed alarm
Of savage strife doth sound, and bids each
 Christian arm!

" The Indians, with Philip at their head,
Are streaming on the town!" And, at the
    word,
She gazes where he points. The sky is red
With newly kindled fires, and, faintly heard,
And chilling every vein, the air is stirred
With sounds of savage shouts, that nearer
    draw,
Then die, then rise again;— dread sounds
    that spurred
Her to escape! They came, as might the roar
Of fitful waves that beat upon some distant
    shore!

She wastes no words, nor sheds one idle tear,
Her woman's soul asserts its inborn power.
She tarries but to seize the thing most dear
To her: 'twas but a drooping, withered flower
Of eglantine, a treasure since the hour
When Wilmot gave it her! And in her breast
She hides it. Now no longer need it cower
Or droop, when near to such a heart 'tis
    pressed!
And then she hastens to the road to join the
    rest.

Her father takes his flint-lock from the nail,
And hastens to the team, and once again
The creaking wagon moves. Once more the veil
Of dust about them grows. The horses strain
Each nerve for greater speed. With loosened rein,
And straightened necks, and nostrils opened wide,
They onward press toward the pleasant plain
Whereon the village lies. The sun doth hide
Behind the western hills, with blood-red color dyed.

And on they hasten through the startled town;
The alarm has spread; and o'er the parching road
Press hastening, their figures freighted down
With hurried salvage from each loved abode,
Both yeomen young and old; each bears his load
Of household treasures. Mothers, by the hand
Lead frightened children, and the duty owed

To those whom age and sickness hath un-
    manned
For troublous scenes like these, though bur-
    dened, none withstand.

The crowding, hurried steps of all are turned
Toward the garrison; and as the light
Of day doth fade, the flaming roofs seem burned
Upon the hills more angrily and bright,
Red wounds upon the bosom of the night!
And nearer and more frequent comes the
    sound
Of hostile shouts, that spurs the hurried flight
Of all who hear it, while the flying ground
Grows heavy, and doth seem to hold them
    clogged and bound!

In little straggling bands, from every side,
They hurry in, with faces pale and worn,
And through the wooden fortress doors, thrown
    wide,
They silent pass; and when the bolts are
    drawn,
And all at last are housed, some, overborne
By sore fatigue, in vain seek needed rest

In troubled sleep, or sit apart and mourn
Their homes in tearless silence; while some, blessed
With stronger souls, essay to cheer each shrink-
 ing breast!

In one long, narrow, dimly-lighted room,
They gather; most are silent, and few dare
To speak in aught save whispers. A dull
 gloom
Doth settle over all. The very prayer
The minister doth offer for God's care
And kindly shelter in this hour of need,
Though followed from their hearts, yet seems
 to bear
No reassurance to their souls, or lead
Their hearts to hope, or bid their fear-bound
 breasts be free!

For all too well they know the cruel fate,
That, if o'erborne, awaits them, young and old,
And had, ere this, been theirs, had savage
 hate,
So long pent up, a few short hours controlled
Itself, and not betrayed by overbold

And o'er-precipitate attack, ill-planned,
Its unripe purpose. Sturdy hearts grow cold,
That knew not fear, and lose their used command
At thought that such dire lot had been so close at hand!

The short alarm, the urgent, hurried flight,
Has served to banish every other thought
From out the breast of Charity, and blight
The recollection of all else; and naught
Of Wilmot, or her love, has once been brought
To mind till now, when in her heart doth burn
The sense that when he left her, sad, distraught,
He promised for to-night, his quick return!
And now his danger fills her soul with deep concern.

For even now toward the 'leaguered town,
Unwarned of peril near, he doubtless rides!
Her startled heart doth sink, deep freighted down
With self-reproach, and sore dismay abides
Within her breast. The thought itself decides

Her course! It may not be e'en now too late
To warn and save him. Noiselessly she glides
Unnoticed from the room. Nor doth she wait
For further parley with herself, but follows
    Fate!

She hastens, trembling, toward the close-
    barred door,
And finds it guarded; yet she doth not stay,
But bids the unwary sentinel withdraw
For further orders from the elders gray,
Who bid him to attend without delay.
And scarcely has he gone, ere she doth strain
To lift the oaken bar which blocks her way,
With nervous, hurried hands, and once again
She stands beneath the sky, with fevered heart
    and brain.

She seeks the shadowed skirting of the road,
And for an instant pauses to array
Her circling thoughts, and then her love doth
    goad
Her on to flight. No longer may she stay;
For now, from out the garrison, the play
Of moving lights, that, gleaming here and
    there,

Pass and repass, and voices loud, betray
Her absence known, and, with a silent prayer,
With stealthy tread she steals away with
    noiseless care!

She casts no look behind, but hastens on,
And holds the tangled way, all overgrown
With weeds, and birches showing weird and
    wan,
A matted path, with briars thickly strewn,
Which borders on the road, where, softly
    thrown,
The moonlight rests. The voices fainter
    sound,
That loudly to her ear but now came blown,
And, as she faster flies, grow hushed and
    drowned
In sad, soft whispers from the breeze-stirred
    trees around.

Too well she knows the urgent trying part
She has to play; yet, with such end in view,
She values not the toil, nor loses heart
At blanching thought of crowding dangers new
And dread that press around. She dares to do

And die, if need be, in so sweet a cause!
A happier lot it were by far, to woo
Kind death, for sake of him her soul adores,
Than live unloved, to nurse a love her pride
      deplores!

Two rough-made roads lead from the garrison,
The one through woods, the other through the
      town,
And, widely spread, unite once more upon
The distant highway, dusty, bare, and brown,
With frequent travel, that winds bleakly down
The hills toward Boston. Here doth lie alone
Her hope that even now success may crown
Her heart's wild purpose, and with this hath
      grown
Another sweeter hope, she scarce doth dare to
      own!

Can she but reach and warn him to avoid
The more frequented road, she need not fear.
The fires, high reaching, mark the foe em-
      ployed
Within the town! The woodland way lies
      clear,

But yet the other is the one more near
To touch the highway. One short moment's
    gain
Is life, may be, to him she holds most dear.
That path is hers! No woman's fears restrain.
The choice is scarcely weighed. This only
    course seems plain.

And thus resolved, she leaves the covert green,
To hasten on the grass-grown travelled way,
And holds the beaten path that runs between
The furrowed wheel marks, till the village
    gray
Beneath the moonlight shows, when she doth
    stray
Once more within the shady coppice near —
She falters not, nor gives one thought to
    weigh
Her danger dread, but ever, bright and clear,
Her purpose shines before, to guide her on
    and cheer!

But as she nears the fitful, ruddy glow,
That mars the pallor of the moon's cold light,
And marks the vandal work of savage foe,

And notes the drifting cloud of cinders bright,
Float o'er the tree-tops, shriveled by its flight,
And hears so close at hand the baleful sound
Of falling roof-trees, e'en her soul takes fright,
And where the sombre branches darkest frowned,
She hastens thither o'er the mossy leaf-strewn ground.

Anon, through some deep vista of the wood,
Dark, narrow, and quick traversed, she descries,
Where, but an hour ago, a cottage stood,
A glowing ruin, whence doth slowly rise
A spangled smoke-cloud, trailing to the skies.
And, for an instant, as she hurries past,
Wild, dusky figures meet her straining eyes,
Which, where the lurid flames are highest cast,
In maddened revel round about them circle fast.

The mingled sounds of ruin fainter grow,
And now the flame-doomed town doth lie behind,

Yet still she holds the wood, whose branches throw
Their shielding arms above her, close entwined,
Until the path she follows, seems to wind
Towards the beaten way, and once again
She takes the dusty road, and looks to find
Some well-known landmark, but yet all in vain;
No spot familiar doth her anxious gaze retain!

Near by, a smoking heap of rubbish lies!
Once more she looks around with troubled breast,
And now a veil seems lifted from her eyes,
And all grows plain, though darkness doth invest
Her love-lit heart, with this new grief oppressed;
For where had been her home, doth now appear
Naught but a smouldering ruin like the rest!
The funeral pyre of all she held most dear
'Midst old remembrances now rising sweet and clear!

And down her cheek the tears unbidden steal,
As, pausing for an instant, she surveys
This scene of desolation, and doth feel
Her heart grow full to bursting; yet she stays
Not long in such drear reverie to gaze
At this dead home, in idle, dull despair,
But hastens on, wrapped in a troubled maze
Of thought. Once o'er the hill, the highway
    bare
Is almost reached. Her goal shows then distinct and fair!

The dismal roll and murmur of the fire
Grows fainter still! Yet as she flies the place,
Comes, indistinct at first, yet doubly dire
In import, a dread sound, that from her face
Sends back the color! Her strained ear doth
    trace
Afar, yet coming nearer, the faint beat
Of hoofs, that hurry from the town apace.
She tops the hill, and now with fear-winged
    feet,
Doth hasten down the road, in unconcealed retreat.

The highway now is reached, but ere she turns
To enter it, from out the vale behind
Three hurried steeds her anxious eye dis-
    cerns
Bear o'er the hill-top, faster than the wind.
It seems as if some evil hand confined
Her powerless there, and checked her eager
    flight.
She presses on, but terror seems to bind
Her faltering feet ; and palsied with affright,
She strives, though all in vain, to shun the
    horsemen's sight.

With savage, wild halloo, the foe give chase,
And faster, nearer comes the beating tread
Of horses' feet, that speed at headlong pace.
Escape seems hopeless, and her heart grows
    dead,
And pulseless sinks before the prospect dread
That threatens her, while through her whirling
    brain
A thousand thoughts, upon the instant bred,
In tangled sequence pass. A vivid train
Of long-forgotten hopes and fears, of joy and
    pain !

CHARITY.

Her sinews fail! She can no further fly,
And, in despair, sinks fainting to the ground.
She breathes a prayer, and waits prepared to
 die, —
When breaks upon her ear the even sound
Of hoofs that draw towards her from around
A mossy knoll, which near at hand doth rise
Before her, thickly wooded, and doth bound
The moonlit road, and now, with startled
 eyes,
A horseman, coming toward her slowly, she
 descries.

With bridle loose, and head bent on his breast,
As though in deepest thought, he slowly rides.
His face is sad, as though some sorrow pressed
Upon his soul, and absently he guides
His well-trained steed. The roadside shadow
 hides
His down-turned face, but as he nearer draws,
And passes where a ray of moonlight glides
Athwart the road, one glance bright hope re-
 stores
To Charity, and through her breast new cour-
 age pours.

'Tis Wilmot, and she hurries to his side,
And as she flies towards him doth essay
To call aloud, but now her voice hath died
Within her! She can only point the way
With eager, urging hands, as, with dismay,
She hears her hot pursuers nearer draw.
Now Wilmot sees her; hears the echoing neigh
And stamp of hurried steeds! He needs no
    more
To warn him that some near, dread danger is
    in store.

There is no time for words, and little need!
He half divines the truth, and with the
    thought
Leaps to the ground, and lightly on his steed
Helps Charity, and then, with bridle short
In hand, remounts. The horse ere this has
    caught
The sense of peril near; with head held high,
And quiv'ring flank, and tense ears backward
    brought,
He forward springs. The moonlit road doth
    fly
Beneath them, and the trees, like shadows,
    hurry by!

And now they enter on the other way
Towards the garrison ; yet not before
The baffled foe, now pressing close, betray,
By shrill and savage cries, which o'er and o'er
The wooded hills and echoing rocks restore,
That they are seen ; and now begins a race
For very life, while Fate doth seem to draw
Its cruel web of circumstance, apace,
About the flying pair, in narrowing embrace.

By slow degrees, the pressing foemen gain
Upon them ; though the o'erladen steed,
That bears the fugitives, doth onward strain,
With spirit high, and never-flagging speed.
Now Wilmot looks behind, and there is need ;
For close, one better mounted than the rest,
Bears fleetly on, and, far advanced, doth lead
The band, and to his ready bow hath pressed
E'en now a shaft, and draws the bow-string to
    his breast.

Quick to his holster, hurries Wilmot's hand !
A shining barrel points towards the foe.
The horse, obedient, heeds the used command,
That bids him start nor flinch not, whispered
    low ;

Then follow fast a sudden blinding glow,
A sharp report, a stifled cry of pain;
And, as the thin smoke clears and rises slow,
Is seen a plunging steed, with wild-tossed
    mane,
To bear on riderless with loosely hanging
    rein!

The others pause not for their comrade's fall,
But onward press, with maddened hearts on
    fire
For swift and dread revenge. Yet now
    though all
Seems dark about them, and with perils dire
Their way is thronged, a sweet sense doth in-
    spire
The soul of Wilmot, doubts are laid aside
That rose of late to rack his heart, and tire
His brain, and now within him doth abide
A spirit calm to bear whatever may betide.

With Charity close clinging, as he rides,
Her trembling hands light resting on his
    breast,
He would not change for all his life besides

This chance of time and circumstance, though
    pressed
By dangers doubly dread, and each is blessed
With sweet assurance of the love of each,
More clearly far than words have yet confessed,
By some strange influence, that deep doth
    reach
Their souls, more potent far than softest looks,
    or speech.

Far down a long, straight line of moonlit road
They dimly see their goal! And now the
    thought
And hope of life that e'en till now had glowed
But far and faintly hath returned, and wrought
New value for the life thus closely bought.
The pressing foemen onward faster strain,
Lest, even now, the chase avail them naught;
And press their steeds by urging shout and
    rein,
As surely, swiftly, on the flying pair they gain.

Lights dance within the garrison! The sound
Of ringing hoofs strikes on the startled ear
Of those within, and echoes far around.

They, all alive for short attack, outpeer
Upon the night, and, 'neath the moonlight
    clear,
Discern the hard-pressed pair, and, short be-
    hind,
The hurrying foe, who follow fast and near!
A second glance bears to each wond'ring mind
The truth! and Charity's dire peril is divined!

An instant more, and half the ready guard
Out-sally to the road, with arms in hand!
The dread pursuers, riding swift and hard
Upon the curling dust-cloud that is fanned
Towards them, maddened, see the succoring
    band
Press on, and, heeding the outnumbering foe,
Draw rein; and at their leader's short com-
    mand,
With savage shouts retreat, and, as they go,
The echoes swiftly, far and ever fainter grow!

The chase is o'er; and, now, 'midst wondering
    friends,
Who crowd around,—all pale and weak with
    fright,

A very woman, now the peril ends,
Fair Charity doth tremblingly alight,
And Wilmot hears the story of her flight,
From those within, and listening, through his
    heart
A quick succeeding sense of soft delight
And pain and fear, all born of love, doth
    start, —
A mingled, soothing sense, where trouble
    holds no part!

Close guard is kept throughout the weary
    night;
But now the foe, their task of ruin wrought,
And sated with their work, in hurried flight
Retreat, upon the vague, swift-winged report
Of strong relief, that even now is brought
To the beleaguered town, and, ere the dawn,
Each straggling band has fled afar, and naught
Bespeaks the late attack, when breaks the
    morn,
Save where the ruins lie, all blackened and
    forlorn.

In after years, 'neath ancient oaks, which
    spread
Their shady branches o'er an emerald lawn,
Doth Wilmot, seated there, with bended head,
Close to an eager group of children drawn
Around to hear the story, never worn,
Relate how o'er the sea, 'neath other skies,
Their mother, sitting there, had placed in
    pawn
Her life for his; while to his face doth rise
A look of love and trust, she answers from
    her eyes.

# GOODMAN JOHN.

GOODMAN JOHN.

How often doth posterity mistake
The soul and aim of what their sires have
    done,
And with an unearned lustre gild each deed,
And, for some common, human motive plain,
Look far beyond the simple end, to find
Some lofty inspiration to great deeds,
Which sober truth would flout!

          Poor Goodman John,
That, throughout all these years, we've looked
    upon
As more than man, a martyr to his faith,
In that he, tramelled, broke the narrow
    bounds,
The spiritual bars, that curbed his soul

In far off England, and sought freedom here!
This third Saint John, it now comes out, by
    chance,
Was but a poor weak mortal after all!
And much we fear, that deep religious faith,
Though it had burned within him ne'er so
    strong,
Alone, lacked warmth enough to exile him,
And bring him over to this wilderness!

Now, how it comes about, that, from his brow,
I thus have ventured, with irreverent hand,
To bear these holy laurels, worn so long,
Is shortly told. I found, by merest chance,
The simple, inner spring, that moved the man.

'Twas but this blustering, rainy afternoon,
When thought lagged slow, and books seemed
    tame and dull,
An empty, drowsy, spring-time afternoon,
To wile away the sluggish, creeping hours,
I sought that dusty store-room, with old
    chests
And motley lumber choked, which, when a
    child,

Had been forbidden ground, a mystic realm ;
And, by the few dull rays of light that came
Reluctantly, as though afraid to smile,
In face of such grave emblems of the past,
In through the one small window close-filmed
    o'er
With ragged webs and all the grime of years,
I handled faded deeds, and rambled through
The store of printed sermons, thumbed and
    worn,
That roused our grandsires in the days gone
    by ;
Glanced o'er old almanacs, and read therein
The margin entries, in a small, cramped hand,
Of when a calf should come, or crop was
    down,
And, pausing, moralized unto myself,
In narrow, hackneyed strain, of time and
    change ;
Until, at last, from out a brass-bound chest,
I there unhoused this yellow packet, creased,
Almost illegible, that lies at hand
Upon the table there ! A few torn leaves
Of what seem random notes, made long ago,
Stray fragments of a journal, and, besides,

Some six or seven letters, quite as old,
Was all the ribbon, loosely tied, contained.
At first, in careless vein, I glanced them o'er,
But found anon, I had misjudged their worth,
And that I, here, had strangely brought to
 light
The cause, why Goodman John left home and
 all
So many years ago. The real cause!
And dreaming here, before the paling fire,
Fresh from the letters and the journal's leaves,
I have a kindlier, softer feeling far
For Goodman John, now that I know the tale,
The homely, simple story of his heart,
Than had he been for conscience' sake alone
The stern old martyr I had fancied him!

Plain inference supplies the missing links,
Where'er the letters and the journal fail;
While, here and there, a fancy is wrought in
To help the continuity, built on
What must have been; and thus, with this
 premised,
Doth run the tale.

Our scene is 'midst green fields,
And 'neath an English sky. On yon fair
    knoll,
Rich, like the fields around, with new-born
    green,
The farm-house stands, deep shaded here and
    there,
By crisp-leaved ivy vines. A time-worn pile,
With many gables.   Thence a sunny view
Spreads out, of grass land sloping to the
    stream
Which, close hemmed in, runs deep and still
    and dark, —
A rude, stone bridge here spans its sluggish
    tide, —
And, rippling, breaks anon o'er sandy shoals,
And widens out between low meadow banks.
A mile away, the little hamlet lies,
Remote, a busy world though to itself,
O'er which, with even, undisputed sway,
The good squire reigns, who holds his court
    within
The rambling mansion on the hill hard by.
Fair hawthorn hedges skirt the rutted road,
That toward the village winds its sinuous
    length,

From where the farm-house stands we saw but
    now.
And, there, within a roomy rustic porch,
That proffers shelter to each passer by,
As foretaste of the welcome found within,
Upon the settle sits a white-haired man,
And opposite, our hero, Goodman John,
Untitled then, and sitting there plain John!
The rose-vines love the sheltered, homely spot,
And, in a tangled net-work, cluster o'er
The unhewn side-posts, and the straw-thatched
    roof,
And now, fresh budding, perfume all around!
A handsome, stalwart, light-haired man is
    John,
More boy than man, though twenty years and
    more
Have closely knit his frame and rounded him,
Yet left a fresh-toned heart, untaught in guile;
Not guileless from sheer incapacity
And needed strength for wrong! Right pleased
    him best,
And so his life was open, pure, and true,
And this true life he lived with all his strength.
Had he toward evil bent, his strength had
    been

Expended there; 'twas temperament with
    him!
Unlike most worthy workers, he could dream,
And sagely fancy he philosophized, —
Yet work as well as any of the rest
In field or elsewhere. Dearly he loved books,
And had, from childhood; yet he read but
    few,
But those few o'er and o'er, and knew them
    well,
And pondered what he read. A clever lad
The curate rated him, and made him free
With all the books he had, a slender store;
And so John grew, at twenty, to be held
A prodigy, by those who did not read,
And, by himself, less learnèd than when first
He conned a line. A sign he studied well
And to some end.

               The elder has the mien
And same strong features, though deep over-
    lined
With age, of him who sits beside him there.
One sees our hero, when he too grows old.
The day's work o'er, they gossip of the farm,

Until the younger rises to his feet.
Then speaks the father, " Where art going,
    John ?
To court the master's lass, I warrant me ; —
Art weary, lad, so hold at home to-night.
The girl will keep till morrow e'en comes
    round,
And greet thee warmer, that thou lagg'st
    awhile.
Thou art a foolish one, to tag her thus ;
She has a pretty face, I grant thee that,
Yet all thy learning comes to little good,
To bid thee ' Like a face and lose a farm ! '
A musty proverb, lad, yet one for thee !
Thou know'st well, John, that I'll not cross thy
    choice,
I love thee over-well ; but bide awhile,
And look around thee, lad, and know thy
    mind !
If mother wert alive, she'd say the same,
And she knew men and women through and
    through.
' She 's not the wife for thee, John,' she would
    say,
I'm weak, and bid thee only bide awhile ! "

" Thou'lt know Ruth better, father, by and
     by!"
Says John, replying, troubled at the words
His father speaks : " 'Tis not her face alone
That holds me, father; 'tis her heart as well,
Her soul's fresh fount, her life's unsullied
     spring!
There's more, by far, in reading such a heart,
Of wisdom gained, than from a thousand books.
'Tis all the one I've lately read, and yet
I've learned to know its beauties but in part!
My head and hands can earn the bread for
     two,
And, as to wealth, what says philosophy?
It enervates the man, and cramps the heart;
The goal of knaves; the only pride of fools!"

" Ah, John! take thy philosophy to fools!
It is their boasted guide, and dear support!
I know not what thy books may teach thee,
     John,
I have but little learning from that source,
But some small store of sterling steady sense
I have, and that alone doth teach me this,
That thy so-called philosophy should be

A code of fixèd truth unalterable ;
It is the creature of each dreamer's whim !
And changes as the wind ! Each man doth
    hold
Some doctrine made to fit his circumstance !
To-day, the ragged pauper rails 'gainst gold,
But then, to-morrow, note his change of key,
When some stray pounds, by chance, fall in
    his way !
A noble ally hast thou, John, to help
Thee jeer at wealth, in thy philosophy !
Thou art young, lad, in years, though old in
    books ;
And that doth bid me hope thy mood will
    change.
Thou'lt ever find a home here on the farm
For thee, and her thou bring'st here as thy
    wife,
But let thy choice be wise, and weigh it well.
I'll stay thee now no longer. Go thy ways ! "
And now the father rises in his turn,
And on the threshold bids his son good night.

So busy press his crowding thoughts, at first,
In troubled flow, at what his father says,

And then, forgetting this, on dreams of Ruth,
That John, unheeding all the scene around,
Doth start surprised, with scarce a moment
         gone,
To find himself within the village street.
Boy-like, he slackens now his conscious steps,
Lest to the evening loungers at each door,
His haste betray the secret of his heart,
And gives each pleasant greeting back again.
And once, with some who gossip by the road,
Doth force himself to stay, and careless talk,
In idle strain, of needed rain, and grass,
To show them all his thoughts are far from
         love ;
And shortly, this dull, foolish role performed,
Bears on again, and nears the garden gate,
That bars a pretty cottage from the road.
And there, beside her father, sits his Ruth!
Her eyes are turned towards him up the road,
But, as they meet his own, shy droop again,
As though she had, but absent, glanced at
         him,
And seen him not.   Yet when, at John's ap-
         proach,
Her father rises, and with welcome smile

And open hand, doth bid him enter in,
And sit with them, she feigns a coy surprise
To see him there, — a spice of coquetry
Hath Ruth, — and barely rising, as he turns,
Just yields her glowing finger-tips to his.
She sees him hurt at this, and, quick as thought,
So sweetly smiles on him with lips and eyes,
That foolish John forgets all else at once,
And stands enraptured!

     Now to picture her!
Her figure that of budding womanhood,
Of middle height, with carriage straight and
  free,
An oval face, o'erbowed with sunny hair,
And so, of course, blue eyes, large, laughing
  eyes,
That were not deep, and never seemed to
  dream!
A nose and mouth, well suited to the rest,
The first, short, velvet moulded, finely cut,
A trifle upward shaded, and the last
Both small and full, an easy sweetness wore
It was a face that altogether charmed, .
Yet did not satisfy; a scentless flower!

She ever minded well her household cares,
She loved her father, and, in different tone,
Though in no less degree, our hero John,
And then, besides, she loved her father's
  friends,
And such girl friends as she herself possessed,
She could not like, she needs must love them
  all,
Although another's liking might excel
Her love in strength; and all loved her in
  turn, —
Her girl friends, and her father, and our
  John.

John sits upon the door-stone, by the rest,
And, soon, with eyes fixed all the time on
  Ruth,
Her own cast down, she trifling with a flower,
Hears the old schoolmaster talk on and on,
In light discourse, although in earnest strain.
In John's keen interest in what he says, —
He notes this from the silence that John
  keeps, —
He takes delight; 'tis seldom that he finds
So eager-eared an auditor as John,

And he had rambled on another hour,
Pleased with himself, and thinking that his
    friend
Was pleased as well,—in soothing monotone,—
Had not a neighbor tarried at the gate, —
A talker too, a tireless man of words,—
And John, relieved, his fetters thus unloosed,
Proposes, now, ere yet the sun doth sink,
A walk to Ruth, to where the river runs.

She, blushing, smiles assent, and both slip out,
Unnoticed now, so busy runs the talk,
And from the road bear off and enter on
A grassy, rutted lane, that runs between
High banks of fragrant bloom, that now bar
    off
The world; and now through tangled frame-
    work, show
A glimpse of distant mellow-lighted hills,
Mist-capped, o'er some long sweep of waving
    field.

Each knows the other's love, and words seem
    vain
To touch so great a theme, so on they pass,

Unspeaking, save to note some little bird,
That from the hedgerow, startled, flies athwart
Their path, — the good-night whisper of the
    elms,
Or mark some daisy, fairer than the rest;
And, thus the river reached, high on the bank
They sit, and watch its sluggish current flow,
And idly drift their fancies on the tide.

" See, Ruth, how clear and fairly tinged the
    sky
Bends o'er the western hills. The mass of
    cloud,
Chameleon tinted, on the clear sky's edge
Hangs motionless, it seems, and all the more
Brings out its radiant coloring pure and deep.
The westward is the future of each sun,
And may ours prove as spotless and as fair
As yonder crystal stretch of western sky!
We'll take it for an augury, dear Ruth,
Of what our life will be in years to come,
And watch until the last tint faints and dies!"

Ruth smiles at this, but closer draws to John,
This dreaming John of hers, whose dreams she
    loves

As part of him, yet scarce can understand;
And, hand in hand, they turn towards the
 west,
To wait the promise of their life to be.

They note no change, until a fainting breath
Bestirs the heavy, heated air, then dies,
Yet, in a moment, stronger moves again,
To stir the grass, and fret the river's flow.
And, suddenly, o'er all the tranquil west,
The feathery clouds, that until now hung high,
And far aloof, deep sink with inky bulk
To blot the sky and crush the dying day.

Then Ruth looks up with troubled eyes at
 John,
And he, quite grave at first, assumes a smile,
" Ah Ruth! we are rebuked, and justly too,
For doubting what was all too well assured!
Our future rests not on a shifting cloud,
But on a love enduring to the end.
It needs no idle forecasting to say
Our love will last, and while that only lives,
Each day must needs seem brighter than the
 last.

Then both arise, warned by the gathering
     gloom
And rising wind, and silent turn toward
     home.
Yet all despite their haste, ere once again
They reach the village road, the frowning sky
Grows blacker yet with heavy banks of cloud.
An instant's lull, in which the storm takes
     breath, —
And then it sweeps upon them with full
     strength,
Just ere the open cottage gate is reached;
And with its strong arms seizes on the elms,
And holds their branches, straining to be free,
And beats the dust-cloud down itself has raised.

They hasten to the shelter of the porch;
Just noting, as they run, a well-groomed steed,
Hitched to the little paling by the road.
While, ere they enter at the door, appears
The schoolmaster, and, standing just behind,
A younger figure, seeming strange to both,
A face, imbued with power, all weather-
     bronzed,

With unlined forehead, rounded, high not
    broad,
O'er which grew black and lustrous curling
    hair.
The face seems strange, yet something in the
    eyes,
Dark browed and gray, a vague remembrance
    brings
Of one long since familiar to them both.
" I beg ye, Harry, till the shower be o'er
To tarry here!   Ah! John and Ruth at last!"
Thus speaks Ruth's father: " Step inside the
    door.
My daughter Ruth, of whom I spoke but now,
And this is John. Ye went to school with him,
When both were boys; and not so long ago!
And, Ruth and John, this is Squire Headford's
    son,
Ye'll be as soaked as they, man, if ye go!"
Then full his eyes young Headford casts on
    Ruth,
And, looking, yields no loth assent to stay.

All enter then a simply furnished room,
With fireplace broad and deep, through which
    the wind

Now sadly moans, complaining of the storm;
And, to repair the damage of the rain,
Ruth, now retiring, leaves them for a time.

Young Headford talked with ease, and spoke
    of scenes
Of which John liked to hear. Of Oxford life,
For he was fresh from academic shades,
And so discoursed of matters and of men,
And sagely generalized, that honest John
Much marveled at such wide experience
In hand with such few years, and, wond'ring,
    sighed
To find his own life had so cramped a scope.
The man had tact, and John was overpleased
To find his reading was not wondered at,
As was its wont, but taken as of course,
And that his new found friend could talk with
    him,
And not stare open mouthed to find he knew
The books that farmers rarely cared to read.
His tone was cordial, nay, e'en over so,
His warmth, indeed, seemed almost forced at
    times,
And more bespoke an effort of the brain,
Than sympathetic impulse of the heart!

We needs must know, or fancy that we know,
The heart within, to build up love or like;
And often knowledge and a love are one.
So John, who felt he had not compassed yet,
The mould or secret of young Headford's self,
Disliked the man, though he could scarce say
    why.
And when, soon after, Ruth came flutt'ring in,
Fresh clad in white, of stuff of tissue web,
With just a knot of ribbon in her hair,
Her cheeks still glowing from the hurried
    walk,
He caught the glance young Headford cast
    on her;
Of admiration was it? Yes, and more, —
A look that bade 'Ruth flush and droop her eyes,
A bare dislike quick took a warmer hue,
That scarce could be concealed. And when,
    at last,
The sky gave hope of clearing, and the rain
Fell thin and wearily, young Headford rose,
And, mounting, waved good e'en, and rode
    away:
Nor tarried John, but, troubled, turned toward
    home.

The slow days passed, with never-varying
  round
Of homely cares ; and though, each eventide,
John walked with Ruth, he never spoke one
  word
That touched young Headford, "She'll not
  see the man,
Mayhap, for years again ;" thus reasoned
  John,
"It would but vex her if I spoke my thought,
And nothing gained ! I'll e'en forget the
  whole."
And, kindly, nought was said, in turn, by Ruth,
Of that strange chance, which, every morn, had
  brought
Young Headford riding past her cottage door,
At just the hour when, household cares com-
  plete,
She plied her wheel within the shadowed
  porch !
And if he tarried just to 'change a word,
What mattered it to John ? — no harm in
  that !
She needs must talk to John of weightier
  things

Than such as these! — He'd love her all the more
If she spoke less of trifles! Tender Ruth!
And it were far more needless then to say
The thing she scarce acknowledged to herself,
The well-pleased, quicker pulsing of her heart,
When, up the road, she heard his horse's tread,
Exactly as the 'customed hour drew near,
And that, when only once he failed to come,
The morning dragged, and something in her day
Seemed lost, and that she listless sat and sighed.

And so with nothing said, John quite forgot
Young Headford lived, and working, hoped and dreamed,
And every hope and dream had life from Ruth.
Thus, having cause to grieve, he still was glad,
And held these days the best he yet had lived.

Each evening brought him eager to Ruth's
    side.
No longer used she coquetry with John,
And had grown dearer to him, so it seemed;
" I need you, John!" she often said of late,
" Thou art so brave and strong, and I so
    weak!"
And always dwelt upon the coming time
When they should wed and fortune smile on
    John!
And thus in present calm and promised joy,
With nought to break their sweet tranquillity,
Those long remembered happy days passed by.

This clear horizon could not last for aye,
And shortly, thus the first faint clouds arose;
One night, a jot behind the 'customed hour
When Ruth would look for him, John pressed
    along
With more than wonted hurry in his steps,
To save the precious moments by her side,
And, as he neared the cottage, from the gate
Toward him sauntered Ruth, and, by her
    side,
Young Headford!

John half stopped, surprised, while rose,
Renewed tenfold, the old concealed dislike
And vague distrust that bade him shun the
    man ;
And while he hesitates what part to play,
Ruth sees him, and with ready tact descries
His grave, unwonted mien, and knows the
    cause.
" We came to meet you on the way ! " she
    says,
And smiles. Young Headford takes his hand
    perforce,
In greeting cordial, and as though he'd found
The friend he valued most, but John is stirred
Too deeply far to be thus easy won,
And coldly gives his greeting back again,
Nor answers to Ruth's smiles, and when the
    gate
Is reached, young Headford frames a bald ex-
    cuse
Of pressing cares at home, and turns away.

Both John and Ruth stand silently awhile,
For each feels wounded at the other's part,
Yet would not venture, on the moment's spur,
To speak their thought.

At last Ruth, pouting, says,
"Thou drov'st our friend away by frowning so;
What ails thee, John, to-night, thou art not wont
To take this surly mood!"

And John replies,
"The man's no friend of mine, nor should be thine;
Thou hast no call or right to walk with him:
I like him not, he's naught to thee or me!"

"Ah John! he is a willing friend of thine,
And shows it thus. He heard my father say
Thou wert a scholar, and would fain be freed
From rustic cares, to closer con thy books;
And straightway, then, he offers to secure
Thy earnest wish, and money gained to boot!
He has a friend, some twenty miles away,
Who'll take thee for a master to his son,
Where thou'lt have books, and time to read them too!
He would not bid thee hope, until 'twas done,
But now, the thing complete, to save thy thanks,

He bade my father tell it thee to-night;
So blush, John, at thyself, and come within!'

" Mayhap, I sorely have misjudged the man;
This kindly act disarms me quite," says John,
" And if I've wronged him in my thought or
        deed,
I'll make amends!"

    "That sounds like John again!"
Says Ruth, and, smiling, takes him by the
        hand.

Thus came it round, that ere another month
Came rustling in, and mellow Autumn dawned,
John left his home, and had e'en now grown
        old
In hackneyed ways, o'er which to guide his
        charge,
Toward the cloud-veiled spring! Dull paths
        they were,
Thick strewn with bare-boned elements of
        things,
That gave poor promise of the fields beyond!
But John toiled on, and when his tasks were
        o'er,

Found sweet relief in converse with the books
He knew and loved the best, or else would
    dream
Of that bright goal that seemed so near him
    now,
And from the petty stipend that he earned,
Built glowing possibilities for Ruth!
His slender store of pounds grew infinite,
When fingered by his wishes or his love!
And busied thus, the days sped lightly by.

Each week a love-fraught letter came from
    Ruth,
Brought by some traveller who should chance
    that way;
And always grimed and crumpled though it
    was,
From o'er close keeping in the bearer's hand,
John pressed the missive often to his lips,
And read the simple, loving words thrice o'er.

And yet he took these letters, as of course,
Nor knew how much they really were to him,
Until when once a whole week dragged away,
And no word came! The hours hung heavily,

And when he tried to fix upon his books,
He scanned the page, but only read of Ruth.
Thus when another week had almost passed,
And brought no news to him of her he loved,
He framed excuse for absence for a day;
And ere the golden foreglow of the sun
Woke o'er the eastern hills, John sought the
    road,
And turned his steps toward Ruth and home
    once more.

Nor tarries he upon the way for rest;
But when the hamlet once again is reached,
He seeks Ruth's cottage, and doth anxious wait
Upon the door-stone, his first halting place,
Until the door is opened wide at last;—
And then Ruth's father, answering his face,
Ere yet his lips can frame a word, doth say
That Ruth had wandered off an hour before,
Yet would return ere long.

                "And she is well?"
He anxious asks:

           "She seems to miss thee, John.
I've often seen her tears fall fast of late,

And silently, when she has thought none by ;
She's not the same she was when thou wert
    here."
Then John, with few words more, turns
    toward the farm
With promise to return !

                    At eventide,
When once again he gained the cottage door,
Ruth welcomed him, with trembling hand, and
    smile
Wherein a tinge of unsaid sorrow lay,
And drew his chair toward the glowing fire,
For now the nights came clear and frostily.

The master gossiped at the village inn,
And Ruth and John sat hand in hand alone.

" Ah, Ruth! thou hast forgotten me of late!
No letter came ; I feared, yet knew not what ;
And this it is that brings me here to thee."

" I tried, dear John, but had no heart to write!
Thou know'st my love, and why then wouldst
    thou seek

To have me tire thee with o'erfrequent words
On what is known so well, and held so dear!"
And here Ruth drops her eyes at John's re-
    gard,
And vainly strives to check the deep-dragged
    sigh
That memory wrested from her weary heart!

" 'Tis not like thee, to speak thus idly, Ruth!
Thy least fond word is something ever dear,
And brighter and still dearer it becomes
In hallowed repetition from thy lips. —
We must no longer live apart, dear Ruth,
Our lives are now so closely interknit
In love and purpose, that they faint apart,
And crave the holy contact of the soul,
The inner, vital essence of all love!
We'll wed anon, and live upon the farm,
And I'll no longer strive for gain from books,
A barren mine for wealth, it seems, at best,
And here I throw that old ambition off.
Another month and we'll be man and wife!"
And John drew Ruth toward him as he
    spoke,
While she hid deep her face upon his breast,
And wept there silently, and clung to him!

But when he sought to soothe her and to find
The undisclosed reason of her grief,
She answered nought, but drew away from
    him,
And vainly tried, through tears, to force a
    smile,
And sought to draw his mind to other themes."

John rose at last, heart-heavy thus to find
Ruth's soft eyes tear-dimmed, and not know
    the cause,
And she held close to him, as loth to part;
And on the threshold, fixing on his face,
A look of love and troubled doubt and fear,
Made effort once, as though she fain would
    speak
Some hidden, inner thought, but no words
    came,
Then bowed her head, and sighed so wearily!

" Good-night, dear John! When next ye see
    my face,
'Twill bear no grief to fret ye with; no
    tears!"
And when John gained the road, and turned
    toward home —

All grave, and with a strange, dull sense of loss
And loneliness within his troubled heart, —
He turned to see Ruth, still within the door.
The moonlight fell upon her upturned face,
Where dawning marks of pain were dimly
    lined,
While heavenward her tearful eyes were
    cast! —
John took that moonlit picture to his grave!

Again he sought his books, and strove to
    find
Forgetfulness in round of wearying cares;
For now no longer came those fancies fair
Whene'er he thought of Ruth, but, in their
    stead,
Grotesque and gloomy pictures filled his brain;
Yet all in vain, he could not master thought!
And ever came a pale and sorrowing face,
With tear-dimmed eyes before him as he
    read;
And every thought was tinged with some
    dread gloom;
And ever turned each dawning thought to
    her!

Thus each dull day dragged heavier than the
    last,
Until one leaden morning, when the wind
Moaned low and drearily from slaty clouds,
And breathed a vague unrest through all his
    soul,
He left his tasks, and sought his patron out,
And told him of his wish to turn towards home,
And meeting every urgent ground to stay,
With but the simple answer, " I must go ! "
He took his pack, and sought the frosty road !

'Twas late before he got upon his way,
And thus the short, drear day was nearly spent,
When, in the valley just before him, showed
The little hamlet on the river side.
The low clouds darkly hung o'er all around,
And all seemed gray and dead and desolate,
And brought no 'customed, joyous thought to
    him.

The village street seemed empty as he passed ;
No loungers gathered at the garden gates ;
The busy forge, where constant labor plied,
Gave out no ring of echoing hammer-stroke ;

And from the inn, no single sound was heard,
Whence ever, as he passed, was wont to come
A cheerful undertone that spoke content
And drowsy comfort of the guests within!
A deathly blight seemed fallen on the place!

But now the jar of slowly moving wheels,
Not far away, struck on his ready ear;
And shortly, from the hedge-fringed, grassy
    lane,
Wherein so often he had walked with Ruth,
Upon the highroad toward him slowly came
A creaking wagon and a noiseless crowd;
A hush hung over all, and every face
A startled look of some great trouble bore!

And while John stood, deep wondering at the
    scene,
Some saw him there and knew him at a
    glance;
At which a buzzing murmur rose and grew.
The wagon stopped, and then the close-drawn
    crowd,
About it intermingled, came and went
Like busy ants! — But just a moment thus,

And then, the earnest consultation o'er,
The rude wheels turned, and all moved on
    again.

John nears the crowd, yet halts again to find
That old familiar faces turn from him;
And that each eye is dropped at meeting his,
Nor can he muster words to find the cause
That brings together all this pallid train!
He stands bewildered, wondering if he dreams,
Until one, braver, and from that more keen
Than all the rest in sensibility,
A rough man, too, from outward mould he
    seemed,
Draws close to John and lays upon his arm
A spreading, horny hand, not roughly though,
But gently as a mother's touch is made,
And slowly, pityingly, thus speaks at last:
"Thou art a true man, John, and brave I wot,
But thou hast need of all thy strength of heart;
There's bad news for thee, man! Aye, bitter
    news!
It touches all, but strikes thee harder yet!
'Tis hard to speak it, John, a sorry task!
Thy sweetheart, John! Thou know'st what I
    would say!

We found her body by the river bank!
One moment yet, man! Brace thyself and
    look!"

John speaks not; and doth hold the speak-
    er's face
With eyes whence all the light and soul has
    fled;
And then, while o'er his frame a tremor
    passed,
Drew toward the wagon, through the open-
    ing crowd,
With heavy step, and scanned, with haggard
    eyes,
The burden there: his Ruth, with upturned
    face,
From which each trace of pain and sorrow's
    lines
The hand of restful Death had lightly
    smoothed.
Beneath her head some tender hand had laid
A jerkin rough, and, seeming as in sleep
One arm lay lightly bended o'er her face,
And wet and matted lay her silken hair,
Decked here and there with sprays of river
    weed.

John coldly looked, and gave no single sign,
By word or passing shadow of the face,
Of all the sore, dull sense that numbed his
    heart, —
His sorrow lay within, too deep and dark!
But when at last before the cottage gate
The wagon stopped, John checked each will-
    ing hand
That fain had helped him, and with reverent
    care
Bore in his arms alone the yielding form
Of her but now he thought of as a bride,
And laid her lightly, tenderly within!

Then, as he slowly turns to move apart,
To 'scape the gaze and pressure of the crowd
Which follow close, comes thrust into his hand
A scrap of folded paper, closely sealed!
He looks and sees Ruth's father by his side: —
"It is for thee, John! 'twas this morning
    found
Within her room;" and here he fails for
    grief.

John breaks the seal, and reads with throb-
    bing brain

These parting words, in Ruth's strained, girl-
    ish hand :
" Farewell, my love ; I dare not, cannot live
To meet thy trusting, tender eyes again,
And know myself so false, so darkly lost,
And thee so true ! Ah ! had I heeded, John,
Thy timely word that bade me shun that
    man !
Forget me, thus unworthy of thy love ;
Or, if in time thy memory should recall
Some clouded thought of me, deal gently then
In judgment of my sin, and if thy heart
Can open to my prayer, forgive the one
Who once had dared to call herself thy
    Ruth ! "

He reads the paper over once again,
Ere yet the full, dread import of the words
Strikes to his heart ! And, then, with bended
    head,
Crushed by the truth the letter has disclosed,
He stands a moment motionless, then turns
To where the body lay, and speaks to Ruth,
As though she were not dead, in husky tone :
" In coming time, not now, I can forgive,

But never all the change nor years to come
Can cloud this cruel recollection out!"
And then he passes from the darkened room!

Some direful purpose darkens on his brow,
As eagerly he presses up the road,
Nor heeds the biting of the autumn wind,
So hotly runs the current of his heart,
So fierce the maddened pulsing of his brain,
Wherein doth dwell but one hard vengeful
    thought,
Whose cruel lustre blinds his struggling soul!

He nears the sombre mansion on the hill,
Wherein the Squire doth dwell; yet at the
    door
A moment pauses, at the whispered voice
Just faintly heard within, that bids him fly
Ere execution follows on his thought!
But then the rushing impulse of his heart
O'ermasters all, and with his clenchèd hand
He beats his echoing summons at the door.

Nor waits he long, for readily swings wide
On noiseless hinge, the hospitable oak,

And he who waited for his word within,
Starts, glancing at the stranger's pallid face
And sunken eyes, turned heavily afar
Toward the thickening night. John noted
    not, —
So eagerly his circling thoughts swept on, —
The open door, till startled by the voice
That asked his errand there!

        " Young master's gone "—
The man says, answering his half-formed
    words —
" To foreign lands, these two weeks since and
    more!"
Then John turns slowly, silently away,
And aimless now, makes toward the road
    again.
But soon his limbs grow heavy, and his brain
Is darkly filled with some dread impotence
That clouds out thought, till by the hedgerow
    bare
He prostrate sinks and yields up conscious-
    ness!

For weeks John tossed upon the sunless sea,
The waste, wide-stretching, 'twixt the shadowy
  shores
Of life and death, till slowly drifted on,
By kindly currents, back to health and
  strength;
And then they broke to him with tender care,
The tearful story of his father's death,
O'erborne by all the sorrow of his son!

Then, with this last bond broken, all his heart
Turned heavenward, to things immutable;
And this new passion flooding all his soul,
He chafed beneath the narrow, cramping yoke
Of form and close knit dogma of the church;
And hearing of a little band, who held
What seemed a purer doctrine to his soul,
And sought asylum far beyond the seas,
He sold his all, and threw his lot with theirs!

Within his journal's leaves of aftertime,
Grows frequent mention of a pleasant name,
A name the daughters of our race still wear.
And, farther on, I chanced upon this rhyme
In Goodman John's own clear-wrought
  rounded hand!

AN APRIL RHYME.

I.

The clouds hang dark and low ;
The leafless trees, and dead brown earth,
A lifeless prospect show,
A prospect full of woe !
Yet something in the air gives birth
To summer thoughts of green,
A something all unseen,
A breath that speaks of buds and bloom,
And song of birds in store !

II.

We feel the earth but feigns
The dreary face of shriveled death,
And that the hot blood strains
E'en now within her veins,
And that anon her od'rous breath
Will fan to life the flowers !
She rests through all these hours,
That when she smiles and breaks the gloom,
We'll know her worth the more !

III.

When hearts seem dull and cold,
And trouble's blast doth chill the breast,
Cease not this thought to hold;
And with it rest consoled.
Then hear that whisper blest,
That voice within, which says,
" Heed not these troublous days,
Nor let thy soul with cares consume!
Thy summers are not o'er!"

www.ingramcontent.com/pod-product-compliance
Lightning Source LLC
Chambersburg PA
CBHW020127170426
43199CB00009B/665